Let's go to
NEPAL

Keith Lye

Franklin Watts

London   New York   Sydney   Toronto

Facts about Nepal

Area:
140,797 sq. km
(54,362 sq. miles)

Population:
17,422,000

Capital:
Kathmandu

Largest cities:
Kathmandu (235,000)
Biratnagar (94,000)
Patan (80,000)
Bhaktapur (48,000)

Official language:
Nepali

Religion:
Hinduism (90%),
Buddhism, Islam

Main exports:
Grains, jute, timber,
oilseeds, ghee (a kind
of butter), potatoes

Currency:
Rupee

Franklin Watts
12a Golden Square
London W1

Franklin Watts Inc.
387 Park Avenue South
New York, N.Y. 10016

ISBN: UK Edition 0 86313 718 0
ISBN: US Edition 0 531 10557–1
Library of Congress Catalog
Card No: 87-51702

Typeset by Ace Filmsetting Ltd.,
Frome, Somerset
Printed in Hong Kong

© Franklin Watts Limited 1988

Maps: Simon Roulstone

Design: Pritilata Chauhan

Stamps: Harry Allen International
Philatelic Distributors

Photographs: Neil Ardley, 3, 4, 5, 7, 10,
14, 16, 18, 24, 25, 28, 29, 30; Chris
Fairclough, 8; Hutchison Library, 11;
Keith Lye, 6, 12, 13, 15, 17, 19, 20, 21, 22,
23, 26, 27, 31

Front Cover: Neil Ardley
Back Cover: Neil Ardley

The Kingdom of Nepal is a beautiful,
landlocked country in Asia. It is
bordered by India and Tibet in
China. The world's highest mountain
range, the Himalayas, covers much
of Nepal. The Himalayas are called
the "Roof of the World". Nepal has
eight peaks which are more than
8,000 m (26,504 ft) high.

Annapurna in Nepal is one of the world's highest mountains. It is 8,078 m (26,504 ft) high. It was first climbed in 1950. The Himalayan peaks are a challenge to the many mountaineers who visit Nepal every year.

Dhaulagiri, west of Annapurna, is an even higher peak. It is 8,172 m (26,810 ft) high. Few people live in the mountainous parts of Nepal, because the long winters are bitterly cold and the short summers are cool.

Sheltered valleys lie in the foothills of the Himalayas. The Kathmandu valley is a fertile region. About two-thirds of Nepal's people live in this valley. The valleys have a cool climate, with heavy rain in summer.

A low-lying region, called the Terai, is in southern Nepal. It is a hot, wet region, with thick forests and steamy swamps. Farmers grow such crops as rice and sugar cane. About a third of Nepal's people live in the Terai.

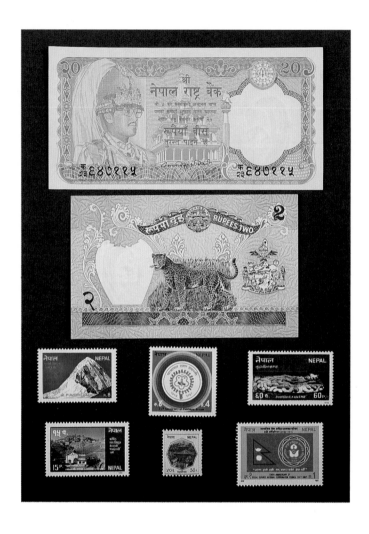

The picture shows some stamps and money used in Nepal. The main unit of currency is the rupee, which contains 100 paisas.

WORLD
MAP

NEPAL

HIMALAYAN

MOUNTAINS

CHINA (TIBET)

Dhaulagiri ▲ ▲

NEPAL

Annapurna

Everest

Terai

Pokhara ●

▲

Kanchenjunga

▲

Kathmandu

Chitwan
N. P.

● ●Bhaktapur

Patan

Terai

Biratnagar

INDIA

INDIA

●

BANGLADESH

9

About 36 languages and dialects are spoken in Nepal. Ethnic groups include the Gurung, Newar, Tamang and Sherpa, who are great mountaineers. A Sherpa, Tenzing Norgay, and a New Zealander, Edmund Hillary, were the first to climb Mount Everest, the highest mountain in the world.

10

Nepalese soldiers are called Gurkhas. Many Gurkhas have served in the armies of Britain and India. They are known for their bravery. Gurkha soldiers served in both World Wars. They also took part in the Falkland Islands conflict in 1982.

People of Indian and Tibetan
origin also live in Nepal. Many
Tibetan refugees settled in Nepal in
the 1950s, when Chinese troops
occupied Tibet. The picture shows a
Tibetan Buddhist shrine at
Jawalkhel, near Patan.

12

Kathmandu is the capital of Nepal. It was founded by the Newars in AD 723. It became the capital in the late 18th century, after the many small kingdoms in the area had been united to form the modern country of Nepal.

The Royal Palace is in central Kathmandu. But the King of Nepal now lives in another, modern palace. King Bavendra heads the government. He can veto laws passed by the National Panchayat (or parliament).

About nine out of every ten Nepalis are Hindus, but many Hindus follow a mixture of Hindu and Buddhist beliefs. There are also some Buddhists and Muslims. Nyatapola temple in Bhaktapur is the highest in Nepal.

Durbar Square in Patan contains many temples and religious monuments. Only seven out of every hundred people live in cities. The rest live in the countryside. Many people live in cities but work on farms nearby.

Flat land is scarce in Nepal. Farmers have built step-like terraces on valley slopes to create fields. Farmland covers 16 per cent of Nepal, and grazing land covers 14 per cent. Farming employs 93 out of every 100 workers.

Grains, including millet, rice and wheat, are leading crops. This field of millet is near Pokhara. Nepal is one of the world's ten poorest countries. Because of poverty and disease, the average life of a person is only 47 years.

18

Most farming is done by hand. This picture shows farmers threshing wheat in central Bhaktapur. They have carried the sheaves of wheat into the city. Nepal exports farm products. It imports fuels and manufactured goods.

Some farmers keep livestock, including buffaloes, cattle, sheep and goats. Hindus regard cattle as sacred animals and do not kill them. Cows wander through the streets of Kathmandu and often eat the vegetables on display.

Nepal has some factories which produce goods for everyday use, such as pottery, food, cigarettes and shoes. There are also jute, sugar, cement and iron factories. But industries employ only one out of every hundred workers.

Many countries give aid to Nepal.
Nepal is building roads, improving
health services and starting new
industries. Nepal has few resources,
but several hydroelectric power
stations have been built on the rivers.

Nepal does not have enough schools and teachers for all its children. New schools are being built, but about four out of every five people in Nepal cannot read or write. This school is at Jawalkhel, near Patan.

Nepal's population is increasing quickly and the country lacks enough services to look after its young people. Another problem facing Nepal is that only 58 per cent of the people speak the official language, Nepali.

Most houses in Nepal are made of
brick or stone. The walls are thick to
keep out the cold. In villages, many
of the houses are small but larger
houses are common in the cities.

Street markets provide fresh food
for shoppers. Many stalls in the
central parts of cities are set up on
the steps of temples. People often use
spices when cooking their food. Many
Nepalese dishes are similar to Indian
ones.

The Nepalis are religious people. They have many religious festivals. The chariot in the picture is used to carry a depiction of a god, Machendra, around Patan (usually in May). Machendra is regarded as a god of rain and plenty.

Nepal is a remote country. But it attracts tourists. In 1984, about 177,000 tourists visited Nepal. Some tourists go on treks through Nepal's spectacular mountain regions. They walk for about five to six hours a day.

Groups of people go on treks lasting several days. Sherpas and other Nepalese porters carry the equipment, tents and food. People who go on treks must be fit and prepared to sleep in simple rest houses or tents.

The Terai has plenty of wild animals, including leopards, tigers and rhinoceroses. The Chitwan National Park near the Indian border attracts many tourists. Visitors can see the wildlife from shelters, or hides, or from the backs of elephants.

One of Nepal's tourist attractions is a flight along the Himalayas to see the world's highest mountain. Mount Everest is 8,848 m (29,028 ft) high. It is on Nepal's border with Tibet. In the picture, Everest is the mountain just above the tip of the aircraft's wing.

Index